WALKING IN GOD'S PRESENCE

CONTENTS

STUDENT ARTWORK

Acknowledgments

Patti Murphy for bringing this book to a reality.

Pat and Nancy O'Malley, Jerry and Alice Hoffberger, William Sullivan, and George McManus for the financial support to make this book possible.

Victor Janishefski for directing the art work.

The students of Calvert Hall College's Art Department.

Mary Page Sater for her time and guidance.

Brother Kevin Stanton, F.S.C. for his support and words of encouragement and the gift of his friendship and brotherhood. The students who have touched my life in profound ways to reveal God's daily presence to me.

Brother Jeremy McNamara whose inspiration gave me the life of a Christian Brother and made all things credible.

My sister Angela and my brother Bud whose love and humor brightened all my days.

❧

The proceeds from the sale of
Walking in God's Presence
go directly to the
Calvert Hall College
Tuition Assistance Program.

❧

Cover photo by: Virginia E. Brown

INTRODUCTION

*T*his is a small collection of poems in the form of journal entries. They are, in fact, responses to persons and events in my life that strongly mirrored for me the presence of God. As I reread them, I can trace special moments when God spoke His words to me in the form of people and daily events. They reflect times when I was listening and "in touch" with His Spirit, breathing inspiration. I see life as a series of moments when God invites us to come into His presence and the most common way in which He makes His presence felt and actually speaks to us is in the goodness of other people. Looking back now at some of my earlier experiences I realize that God was always close to me but I wasn't always close to Him. I wasn't looking or listening for His ways of communicating. But in my later experiences I feel that through His good graces I have been attuned to His "wavelength," realizing that quite often in the course of a day He is with me and conveying special messages of love, comfort and challenge. Life takes on added meaning when one walks in God's presence. It changes perspective and "frame of reference." As St. Julian of Norwich often said, "God wishes that all shall be well for us." When we believe this and live it, we welcome each day as an opportunity to be filled with love for others and for God in them.

It is my hope that these reflective poems will help others to develop an awareness every day of God's love for us in our uniqueness and that He "walks beside us" on our journey to find Him.

Let us remember that we are constantly in the holy presence of God!

I owe everything to the Christian Brothers, some of whom are the greatest men one could ever hope to meet this side of heaven. Yes, God is indeed present in our world and very frequently, He calls us into His presence through the goodness of other people. I have found Him in my brothers and colleagues as well as in my students. In all of the everyday happenings of my life He is there calling me to greater spirituality.

This collection is an attempt to make His presence felt in the lives of all who read about my personal journey through poetry. The words and images are God's made real through His spirit moving in my daily encounters. They affirm my belief that God spiritually empowers each one of us through His presence in other people.

Brother Kevin Strong, F.S.C.
November 1996

Brother Kevin Strong at Biscayne Bay in Miami, Florida 1963.

The Return
....

Slow the pace
it seems
to return home.
Long is the journey
to my Father's house.
Migrant geese
spell "home"
across the evening sky.
You've come full circle.
Now you are home.

Peace at last!

At Carroll
June 10, 1987

Gift of Joy

....

Persons can be gifts too.
Think of laughter, humor, joy.
All that makes the person real.
Things often taken for granted.

But a life is a gift to us
That lightens burdens and pushes
Us through the shadowy parts.
Remember Matt - the power of presence.

He sauntered, ambled and ran,
Filled with a light-hearted vigor
Bringing smiles with his style
Of warming hearts and lives.

He used his gift to be a gift
And we are lifted to a level
Of transformed love and warmth.
Gifted hearts still smile.

God brings His own life
Into ours through people.
Don't miss the message He sends.
Matt, God's word, spoke LOVE.

Matt's 2nd Anniversary of his Homecoming
January 12, 1989

Matt Bevenour died as a result of an
automobile accident while attending his
freshman year at Temple University.

St. John Baptist de la Salle

Prayer

....

Solace to our troubled waters,
You walk upon the waves of pressing needs.
We look up occasionally and,
like Apostles, plead,
"Lord, save us; we perish."

You awaken to put all things right,
to ask in dulcet voice,
"Where is your Faith?"
And we are reassured
Because we sense Your power,
Your calming presence.

As we look to You, Lord,
Look back to us,
with glances of love and understanding.

Let us hear You say,
"Fear not at all -
see I am here. I am with you now."

At Carroll
June 5, 1989

Brian J. Sette, *Calvert Hall Class of '98*

The Welcome

Brother Kevin Strong, F.S.C.

Waters of Siloe

....

These are the waters of Siloe
That flow in silence,
Quenching waters
Springing from quiet, stored up.

In times of exile
from inner space,
Waters of Siloe well up
from deep within
To restore calm;
Peace-filled estuaries
That the world knows not.

Inner fountain,
you are the fruit of
contemplation.

You are God-given.

When vessels empty,
Silence waits for your torrents
To bathe in God's waiting
grace-flow.

Daylesford Abbey
June 28, 1989

Refresh Me, Lord!

Mourning doves chant the office of
  interrupted quiet
  on a silent afternoon.

Daylesford is serene space
  where I am found
  by the Lord of nature.

Green grow the woods of cloistered deer
  and I am surrounded by
  sounds of Nature's summering.

In this lush countryside God's gentle winds
  announce "freedom." Worldly cares are
  foreigners in this strange country of
  resonance and rustic hue.

And I am humbled by the Lord's largesse
  as He plays upon my heartstrings.
  His melody of trust.

I am Your obedient servant, Lord.
  I come to know Your will for me -

I open my buds to embrace
  the refreshing dew of grace,
  God's gift.

And I am happy!

Daylesford Abbey
June 28, 1989

Woodcut by Helen Siegl

Gift of Self

....

Make my life an open page, Lord,
    to write your message of love upon
        for the world.

Let it say in Your most simple,
    yet beautiful, language,
"Kevin, my son, used his gifts for others
    in order to please Me."

Then, Lord, You may want to add -
    "I am proud of his efforts
to use talents to say to Me,
    'All that I am, I give back
        to you in love.'"

And I would say further -
    "Your grace was sufficient
for me, Lord - it was my pleasure
    serving You, Lord of the gift-giving."

Daylesford Abbey
June 28, 1989

J. Michael Talbott, *Calvert Hall Class of '99*

Ryan T. King, *Calvert Hall Class of '99*

Sleep
....

I read once that sleep knits up
the raveled sleeve of care -
a great image!

Sleep brings restful quiet for
the ever-searching soul.
Day upon day, yearning for God's
fulfillment, seeking surcease,
Sleep is the God-gift that gives balm
to all of life's questions.
Questions cannot all be answered in the
present time -
Some answers can only come with
the unfolding pages of time
in another chapter of my story.

Thanks be to God for sleep, an interim
station, where life's train stops,
only to proceed to a new destination
on the life-route.

Daylesford Abbey
June 29, 1989

To Ponder

....

I wonder how you think of me, Lord!
Is it as I was when You first fashioned me
In my mother's flesh

Or, perhaps, as I grew in childhood,
In the freshness, the unspoiled
    newness of a little boy's wonder?
Did You want to hold me there,
    untainted by life's harsh lessons?

But, I reason, You must love me
    in Your eternal NOW;
yesterdays of wonder, promises, too,
    today's dreaming quests, and
    Your hidden tomorrows —

You surely must view me
    in my totality of essence,
All that You hoped I could become
    and did.

Whatever - Yours I shall always be!

Daylesford Abbey
June 29, 1989

Timothy M. Byrne, *Calvert Hall Class of '98*

Musings

....

Written on my heart
    Are your promises, Lord!
You said, *"Do not be afraid.*
    I will be with you."

As a child might ask,
    "In conflict, Lord?"
"Yes, especially then,
    I will be with you."

"In the loss of loved ones
    and friends, Lord?"
"Yes, I will be close by."

"As the ravages of time
    take bodily toll, Lord?"
"I will always love you,
    even then, my son."

"When evening comes on
    and You call me, Lord?"
"I will open my Father's arms
    to embrace you, son."

"Then I will no longer be afraid."

Daylesford Abbey
June 29, 1989

Brother Kevin Strong at the Christian Brothers Scholasticate in Elkins Park, PA., 1952.

Stephen M. St. Amant, *Calvert Hall Class of '98*

Nature's Own

A family of deer
    frolicked in the evening twilight
        in the orchard
        near my window.

Shadows closed in as they
    awakened to new life,
        as though, napping all day long.

The mother deer stood watch,
    her ears tensed to hear strange sounds.
Three very young fawns skipped and chased
    one another in moss slippers of silence.

This family of five moved in perfect harmony, playing
    off of each other
        in the forest green.

As I prepared to sleep,
    they came alive to the silent
        wonders of falling night.

A provident God cares for man
    in the same manner as for these creatures
        of the wooded glen.

Daylesford Abbey
June 30, 1989

Retreat

To be touched by your gentleness, Father,
    Really touched, graced repeatedly
        during time apart.

You speak to me of wind, breeze
    and storm
Amid scent of magnolia blossoms
    You sent winged messengers
        proclaiming love, peace
        in the heart.

In quiet recesses of my soul,
You whispered words of
    contemplation.

Refreshment, and peace-filled longings
    spoke your name to me.
They said, "Yahweh, the Faithful one,
    is present in my world."

Daylesford Abbey
June 30, 1989

Song

··

To lift my voice
in tones of melody
Is gift and grace
undeserved.

Your touch causes
the symphony,
The soothing strains
of softness.

Only you, Lord
could create song,
Reflections of life
in joy and sorrow.

Let my life be your song,
Full chorus
Of love for life
and shared, heartfelt
friendship.

You come to us
in different guises, Lord,
But You are unmistakable
in song.

At Carroll
July 6, 1989

Colette

....

Fair flower of God's own fashioning,
Colette was His surprise.

Kept for me until now,
Joy is her message
Late though her coming be.

Goodness finds itself
though it travels
Winding pathways.

Her parents' blessing,
Colette is the symbol
Of love shared.

Thoughtful, kind of heart,
Her fragrance touched
my spirit, as a daughter's might.

God be praised in Colette,
miracle of His spirit
Speaking words
of promise for His future.

At Carroll
July 11, 1989

Colette Riegler was a student, later a nurse,
from Archbishop Carroll High School, in Radnor, PA.

Bring Me Home

Today, at Mass,
  I heard You say,
*"Home is where
  the heart longs to be."*

All around are signs
  of Your loving me -
I get a glimpse only
  of home when You, O Lord,
Are near.

Bring me home, at last;
  Let me rest upon
Your heart's beating
  In the end.

As John at your last repast
  leaned upon your breast,
Let me find favor in being
  "At home" in your presence.

Longings of the heart
  so deep
Call me forth from now
  to home,

Always with You
  as one - together!

*Adamstown
July 30, 1989*

Forgiveness

....

I release my hurts
    for Your healing
Let me be balm
    for others' indiscretions,
Not judge.

If I ask your cleansing touch
    for me,
Let it also cover
    others' dark,
I ask sincerely.

In the measure
    we release old ire,
To us it shall be
    shown as well.
Your mercy swells
    within our hearts.

As You see me
    in the sum total,
Let me cast forgiving eyes
    on others' deeds! Amen!

Adamstown
July 31, 1989

Brother Kevin Strong, F.S.C.

The Good Shepherd

Indwelling

At my center
  You wait to be called forth.
I never fully know
  just how,
only that You are here.

I am overwhelmed,
  loved, cherished and
empowered to release You
  for good in others'
lives and my own.

As in a monstrance,
  raised high and shining,
You are carried in
  Life's procession.
I do not want You
  to die within
But to raise You up
  lovingly,
To shine through
  my solitary love.

I am caught up,
  embraced by the Power
  at my center -
The power known as Wisdom.

Adamstown
August 2, 1989

Cherished

....

What does it mean - to be cherished?
We all need to be
and seek it night and noon.

It demands much of us
if we are to open ourselves
for service
And bearing another's burden.

There is risk when we reach out
to clasp hands held out in offering.
Be prepared for listening.

"Cherished" is earned
by time's investments,
To look for the lonely heart,
the lonely place
And fill it.

When we spend our gifts
for others' empty places,
When we bend to receive "old hurts"
We allow for loving,
We learn what "Cherish" means.

Adamstown
August 4, 1989

Look for the Light

....

We are drawn, like moths,
    to the light.
Be it beacon, sunset or candle,
        Our lives search
        for transformation in the lucent.

We are today's children,
        always cursing darkness
By bearing the beams within us
        to become children of the light.

God sees our need
        and suns us into twilight's gold
and dawns of amber hue.
        Daylight to night sky,
God spoils us with His energy.

Light means life and loving;
        at our center where God dwells,
shinings yearn for release,
        for dispelling shadowed
            corners and shaded eaves.

Adamstown
August 6, 1989

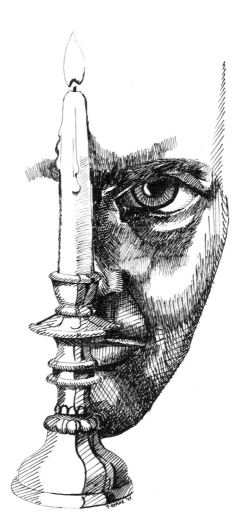

Timothy M. Byrne, *Calvert Hall Class of '98*

Awesome

Your world shines forth
    even amid the squalor.
In ghettos, slums and back streets
    Your sun warms all;
Your breezes cool even the poorest.

Blossoms scent the wayside
    for rich and poor as well
And leafy trees shade all persons
    from the heat of summer's brilliance.

Your largesse is all around us;
    We need only to open our eyes
And raise our awareness
    to our spendthrift bounty,
Only a fingertip away.

Lord of the harvest,
    Lift our clouds so we may see
Your awesome wonders which bathe us
    In your wealth, all for us
to savor and to be steeped in.

At Carroll
August 31, 1989

Dan

....

Into my life You sent
    the smiles of Dan
To lighten the burdens
    of a winter's day.

Unaware of his impact,
    his ebullience bought
Surcease from monotony
    and daily humdrum.

Many overlooked
    his sterling insights
and gifted power
    of simplicity.

Humbly he sees not
    the endowment of
God's generous touch
    of talent.
Dan, you are empowerment!
    God calls you to awareness
of roads less-traveled.
    You need only God's healing stroke
for scales to fall.

Look, see and live!
    Choose life and make
Your precious mark
    upon God's world!

At Carroll
August 31, 1989

Dan Langan was a student at
Archbishop Carroll High School in Radnor, PA

Your Day is Gift

Your day is gift to each of us,
    Space to fill with love,
The love You brought to our ken
    Through Calvary's drama.

Let us see with Your eyes
    The good we can be and do,
To banish others' lack of love
    and light.

As a shining, You pervade
    Our shadowed parts and open us
Much like roses to bathe in
    Your powerful, graced love-shine

Beam out the dark
    And let Your brilliance
flame out from us;
    Fire for your people in need of peace!

At Carroll
September 4, 1989

Hero

....

Life freely given
    for others
Not tallying costs
    but gladly
Spending the gold
    of energy!

Being able to say,
    "Not my will"
And meaning it.
    "And if it be possible,
Let this chalice pass."

More importantly,
    Internalizing
"Thy Will be done!"
    Then, doing it.

Can this be the stuff
    from which hero comes?
Lord, in truth,
    You are our mold -
The Ideal that spells
    Saint
in human terms.

At Carroll
September 28, 1989

Shepherd

Pasturing in peace,
You have called me
to earth's edge
    for stillness.

You speak your words
of shepherding
Against the sea's
murmurings.
And I am refreshed
hearing Your promise
    Of presence in my world.

Beside still waters
You lay before me
    a brighter and stronger me.

Be with me, Loving Pastor,
and search me out of dark,
out of the way places
    Where You are not!

Avalon
October 12, 1989

Tommy

···

Having no son of my own,
    Tommy became Your bonus gift,
A sign of Your love for me.

His quiet gentleness,
    ready smile and personal goodness
Calls me often into Your presence.

Seeing Tommy is seeing
    something of You.
His warmth of caring
    speaks Your words of
        Love and fidelity.

Tommy comes to me
    with only the gift-tissue
of simplicity - your markings,
    "To Kevin with Love."

At Carroll
October 16, 1989

Tommy Dunn was a student at Archbishop Carroll.
I later sang at his wedding. We are lifelong friends.

J. Michael Talbott, *Calvert Hall Class of '99*

Growing Old

In my mind,
    I see an ageless reflection
Just me, even as I was
    when I was ten.

But years of journeying back
    to God from whence I sense
I did come, brought changes.

Changes more internal
    than facial ones or bodily
markings of time's bruises
    and weathering away!

"Who are you
    and why have you come?" I ask.
In answer, "from God
    and I am His NOW."

At Carroll
October 16, 1989

What is Love?

....

What is love?
     Energy or a power
coming from within,
     Somehow from God at my center.

Love is released for good,
     For lightening a burden
or a troubled brother or
     a suffering sister.

Love transforms others
     and in so doing
Rubs off the tarnish
     from darkened silver
Built up around the human heart.

Love energizes us,
     Gives us God-like perspective
To make the world a brighter place.

At Carroll
October 26, 1989

Bryan Barry Dunn, *Calvert Hall Class of '97*

40th Anniversary

··

However did these members from
my past suddenly become old?
In an eye's twinkling, they became
Wrinkled and turned gray.
Impossible! Only a day ago
we were all young and vigorous,
Anticipating a promise of success
at whatever we wanted to try.

Now, two score have gone by
and time has made its markings
On our frames. Only traces of
youthful smiles and slimmer
silhouettes give hints of who we were.

Friendships, though, are held
encased in timeless spheres
just as we were then!
Warm hearts and faithful pledges
of Loyalty say "we are the same."

At Carroll
October 26, 1989

Stephen M. St. Amant, *Calvert Hall Class of '98*

Invitation

....

Not so long ago
    I heard a voice within
Calling me with persistence,
    "Leave all of this and come."

Uncertain, timid and questioning,
    I answered by my response
To the invitation. "A hundredfold
    now, in the present time"
    was the promise.

"And further more,
    eternal bliss."
What does bliss mean?
    The reward that comes from service,
from running toward the mark, pressing on.

You reached out to me and offered
    Eternal happiness.
In faith, I followed You along the Road
    to "NOW" - Your promise fulfilling!

At Carroll
October 27, 1989

Brother Kevin Strong, F.S.C.

Morning Musings

Softly the day unfolds,
        slipping quietly in with
Hushed fog sounds, beginning again
        The quest for meaning.

What does this day say?
        Does it say, "You are
my presence here and now?"
        I think it does.

All that makes me "real"
        becomes Your word today
For all I meet. I am, indeed,
        "Who Am" just as You said.

There is mystery here,
        yet often repeated mystery.
I count on You to sharpen my dullness,
        To see You all around me in Your "todays."

At Carroll
October 31, 1989

Graced Moments

....

Not expected, trimming.
Clipping, stream-lining,
You shaped me in quite a different
way than I would have planned.

Each of us picks, chooses, selects
and rejects. Somehow the Truth
shines forth from all that
we choose in our becoming.

A tapestry is woven,
Yet not always of our choosing.
Whose, then?

Partly mine, but more of Yours
with a Father's care for the children
of His own making.

The Potter used the common clay
But created something new and wonderful
of His own artistry, Something of Himself,
Reflections of His Image.

At Carroll
November 13, 1989

November Alleluia

....

Trees are spokes of wood,
    Soldiers in queues,
Along the edge of fields and lawn.

Strewn about are remnants of
    Summer's greening, now scarlet
and amber and umber.
      Leaves tell tales of life's cycles.

My life, too, reflects
    God's plan of colors.
Youth, the bursting time,
    Life-filled blooming of
God's spendthrift energy.

Then comes mid-life in
    hues of woods and flowers' fullness.
Winter seems imminent as the quiet mauves
    and shadowed grays stand waiting.

Nature's way, preordained.

At Carroll
November 15, 1989

Make Room

....

Today calls,
    "Make room for God."
I look inward,
    for space, for emptying.

God needs room
    if He is to be with me!
A pause, an ear tuned
    for listening for His word.
Make room, make space,
    for grace and presence
For fullness of grace
    when God is invited in.

Always let there be room;
    for joy and peace
Are your gifts in fullness
    When we say, "Come into my house."

And we, looking up, see only You,
    A loving Father.

Jeremy House, Advent Day of Prayer
December 10, 1989

Little Man

....

Smallness, greatness,
and all in one!
This little man, the saintly one,
followed God's small
and humble ways.

Not easy to be the lesser,
always serving and seeking God
In "out of the way" places,
in His small ones.

A great model to pursue -
One who was always
"The foreigner"
both in origin and in his
Humble ministry.
Being small, like Therese,
He found God and greatness
In humility, in patience,
in loving the young, the poor
and the homeless.

Feast of St. John Neumann
January 5, 1990

Departing

....

I remember a quotation
that touched me deeply.
I read it many years ago on
a change of mission, after
six glorious years serving there.

It said, "Love knows not its
own depths until the hour
of parting." It is true.
I feel it deep within me.

Can one love a place?
I love Carroll.
What is Carroll to me
Carroll for me is the young,
the yet-to-be formed ones,
children's lives, carefree
and ebullient.

As I prepare for my leave-taking,
the love I feel for them
is very deep - God's hidden gift
was revealed to me, in the end.
The Youth were His words to me.
"See, how much I love you!"

At Carroll
January 18, 1990

Brother Kevin Strong, F.S.C.

Spirit

....

There is a Spirit
that fills all of our being
With its energy.
We are driven by this
force for loving, being
and giving of ourselves.
God's spirit within,
motivates our movement
Our reaching out to others.
Inspiration gives direction
to all we do for Him, in Him
and by Him.
Great spirit, lift us
to a new level of being.
Raise us above the mundane
to view the larger picture.

And what is the larger picture?
Your will for us
In all our daily encounters.

At Carroll
January 22, 1990

51

Brother Kevin Strong at the Christian Brothers Scholasticate in Elkins Park, PA., 1952.

Beginnings

....

Beginnings mean newness
    and freshness.
It is opening our horizons
    for new visions -
Accepting the gift of awakening.

Letting go of all that went before,
    we are at a new place now.
It is refreshing to know
    we are still developing our
sense of wonder and surprises.

Uncharted waters, beginnings
    need not be feared.
We bring all of our history
    as strengths to face
the unexpected, the new opportunities.

Thank you, Father
    for new beginnings.
Like the seasons, they
    refresh us for new life
and the awe of your creation.

At Carroll
January 25, 1990

Winter Peace

··

Against the backdrop
     of mountaintop grandeur
You were at Your best
     in providing wonderful
winter-magic on trees,
     snow and running streams.

Never before have I seen
     a bluer sky, snow-covered trees
and icicle wonders,
     all created for just our pleasure.

As a Shepherd, You called us
     to the wooded mountaintop
and laid before us Your best
     masterpieces of color and
scenic beauty. We were in awe
     of Your power and your peace.

Lord, you know our hearts
     and our greatest needs. You,
our Shepherd, lead us beside still waters.
     It is You who restores our souls.
        Deo gratias!

Dushore, PA - Shepherds'
Weekend of Prayer
January 29, 1990

Fiat
....

Let it be done, Lord,
    as Your will for me
unfolds. Your grace
    is all about me.

I know your strength
    and wisdom flow
into a heart steeped
    in humility - much like Mary's.

Like morning light
    Your grace brings hope
that your presence and love
    alone can sustain.

I cannot see the future;
    only the "now" greets
my opened heart.
    Your time will hold the "how."

As David, sling in hand,
    I face the giant "unknown."
I am unafraid, shielded
    in your armor of faith and zeal.

Amen.

At Carroll
March 2, 1990

Spring

....

All about me the signs
of change appear.
The sun's warmth
calls forth new life.
Seasons are harbingers
of God's artistic hand
at work in our world;
He surprises with His gifts.

Only He could fill the void
with unforeseen rushes
of His colors and scents,
His unmistakable touches of presence.

God's world is opening
before us and His generous heart
fills all our needs and wants
to overflowing.

Unsought generosity
announces His bountiful presence
and a Provident
abundance of loveliness.

At Carroll
March 15, 1990

Brother Kevin Strong, F.S.C.

Christopher W. Pasko, *Calvert Hall Class of '97*

Colin P. Gause, *Calvert Hall Class of '98*

Resurrection

In quiet, we are reborn.
    All the dead leaves of other years
drop away to make way for the greening
    of branches touched by Spring,
Your spirit.

Our hearts are lifted up to You,
    Father, as sap rises in each stem
to seek the light.
    Energy anew abounds all about us.

Bloom into loveliness our gifts
    yet to be discovered and used
as Your healing presence for
    Life-giving gift to others' shadows.

From the tomb of our sluggishness,
    surprise us with your grace,
Your thrust for renaissance
    and for Your unfolding promises.

We are transformed anew
    each Spring - like cocooning butterflies,
symbols of resurrection
    and another chance to create afresh.

At Rosemont - Day of Prayer
April 8, 1990

Mary's May

....

Motherly tenderness enfolds
    our earth as blossoms
appear all over our land -
    it is Mary's month.
A gentle aura covers
    a world in seizure -
a world longing for wholeness and peace,
    a world thrusting in the dark.

Imperfect ourselves, we see
    God's perfection in Mary,
the pride of humanness -
    She is our shining one.

There is hope for us
    through her prayers as mother.
Her caring for the struggling
    mass of humankind.

Let the blooms and bursts of flowers
    say to us, "Mary is near"
and earnestly transforming our world

At Carroll
May 8, 1990

Joseph P. Cohan, *Calvert Hall Class of '98*

Perceptions

....

How we perceive something
is more relevant, more significant
than what it is
that is perceived.

Failures, as well as successes
are our beacons
to light the way
to deeper understanding of ourselves.

Perspective, simplicity,
service and single-heartedness -
all result when anxieties
and illusions are dispelled.

We need to perceive rightly,
to escape from selfishness,
from personal idolatry -
Faith is our beacon for seeing.

Each day, warm, serious faith,
if embraced with full will,
enables us to listen for God's touch.
Nothing replaces faith
(seeing through God's eyes).

Manresa-on-Severn
July 23, 1990

Dominic A. Terlizzi, *Calvert Hall Class of '99*

Kirk B. Roush, *Calvert Hall Class of '99*

Annapolis

....

History is here, in this place.
The steeple of Old St. Mary's
reaches for a blue sky
between the Naval Chapel
and the Capitol Dome.

The Severn River peacefully meanders
past the Naval Academy
and on its graceful waters
sailboats glide on cool breezes to the Bay.

St. Anne's spire amidst the trees
is witness to tourists
weaving in and out of tiny streets
which empty onto the Harbor dock.

Flags wave freely and strolling vacationers
ease into antique shops.
Midshipmen in summer whites are testimony
to traditions set in motion years before.

Annapolis, you hold your proud head high
for all ages!

Manresa-on-Severn
July 24, 1990

Reflection

....

In a garden
    there is a variety
that speaks to all of life's experiences.
    Differences are important!
A walk along pebbled paths,
    patterns of colors shout
joyful messages that celebrate variety
    - uniqueness reigns.

All that blooms in profusion -
    cosmos, lupines, zinnias,
mirrors of diversity,
    rejoice in unison.
There is wisdom here
    for us to ponder.
Life is a kaleidoscope.
    Calling us to gasps of wonder!

Day of Prayer for Faculty
Nativity Parish Center
September 4, 1990

66

Wise Men

....

We, like the Wise Men,
seek Him still.
His guiding star is faith
in a world without peace.

All about us, chaos draws us
onward in our quests.
If help is to come,
it comes from outside our boundaries.

In the East looms war,
darkening tomorrow's horizon.
As then, in ancient days,
a simple Child is the key.

In our darkness, we yearn
for light - the light of peace.
We look to the Messiah yet,
to restore us to calm.

Let there be your shalom!
The lands you walked
are troubled still.
Let there be no more crucifixions!

Written during the Gulf War.
Calvert Hall College
January 23, 1991

Awaken

....

Heaven is all around us!
Each tree speaks God's name;
every flower is aflame
with the artistry of His hand.
Awaken and see! Come alive -
take off your shoes -
Feel the grass under your feet
and pluck the red-ripe strawberries.

Calvert Hall College
January 23, 1991

Presence

....

Let your presence
Overpower the evil
That sometimes lurks in our hearts
As unhealed wounds of yesterday.

Do not permit shadows
To cover the Light
That Your gifts to us
Can illumine.

Your peace, grace, and
Strength overpower gloom
And jealousy of the gifts we
See so well in others.

Let us be secure in
Who we are before You;
Humble yet strong
In our desire for virtue.
Your goodness is balm
For old wounds and hurts.
"In Your light we see light,"
Transform us for giving life!

Day of Prayer at John Carroll School
March 4, 1991

Where Are You Going?

You ask, *"Where, where are you going?*
        Do you know? Is there an awareness
of your journey? And who will be with you
        and where?"

Space and quiet permit me to ask of you!
        Take time to look about you,
to pause to ascertain the direction.
        Listen for the sounds that call you to "wholeness."

Awareness is of the greatest importance.
        Signs and tokens spell the way!
Elijah felt the gentle breeze, a gift!
        He only listened for God's touch.

O my Lord, let me find you here
        In quiet place and crickets' song.
In flower fields and shady trees
        As birds on wing herald your creative hand.

Look up and sense the strength and wisdom,
        My gifts, which I pour freely
Into your heart cupped with longing
        For the energy of love,
food for the journey.

Faculty Day of Prayer
Nativity Parish Center
September 3, 1991

Brother Kevin Strong, F.S.C.

Peace Be with You

The quiet summer's greening
Sifts through my life -
A time of gifts recalled,
Persons who touched the rim of memory.

A lifetime is passing.
It is time to recall the blessings,
To value God's own presence
In loving relationships.

Each is a precious part
Of friendship's storehouse of gold.
I have been loved by many
And they have shaped my frame.

I am stronger now
Enriched by those who walked with me
Passing into other seasons
of Summer, Autumn and Winter - no longer Spring.

Peace has come through Time's tracings!

Malvern Retreat
August 10, 1992

Bryan Barry Dunn, *Calvert Hall Class of '97*

Brother Kevin Strong, F.S.C.

An Indian Prayer

We pray to you, O Great Spirit,
Whose voice we hear in the mighty wind
And whose breath gives life to all of our world.

We reverence you in the golden sunrise,
the flight of eagles, the trees who give us shelter
And feed us with their fruits for our bodies.

We feel your life-giving being
in the Mother Earth which nurtures the seeds
Sleeping beneath the touch of our moccasins.

Give us strength for the hunt and courage to face
the winds dancing over the snow-covered crags.
Let us not waver when we face the dark forces
unfamiliar to us.

Let us feel your powerful hand behind our bows
And the swift flight of our arrows, as we search
For food for the very young and
the very old among us.

May we care for the rich soil, the yielding fruit vines
And the all-embracing hills keeping guard over our
Peaceful valleys, so that our offspring may have
Them to show their children and grandchildren.
O great grandfather, as we behold You in the purple
hills
Enfolding us, let us come to You with clean hands
And straight eyes, so that our spirits may rest
Among our ancestors in the
Happy Beyond which you
provide for the fulfillment of our spirits.

May all of this come to be!

For Thanksgiving Liturgy
Calvert Hall College
November 15, 1992

Light in the Darkness

John came as witness to testify to the light
Jesus was the light, shining for all to see.
John said that he was not the light but came
Only to announce the light, Jesus.

To those of us who receive Him into our lives
He is the light that shines forth from us.
It is He who empowers us to be light for others.
It is He who spreads the light of Faith.

This Word made flesh, dwelling in our midst,
Reaches out to us in the person of the poor.
If His glory is to be seen in today's poverty
Then we must be the source of His light.

Of His fullness we have all had a share,
Not just for ourselves, then, do we shine,
But that others may bask in this light and be warmed,
Love following upon love, Christ's love shared.

Yes, it is Christmastime again and the words are clear.
They are clear as the crisp cold of December.
He became man and dwelt among us in light of faith.
Can it be said of us, as it was of Him -
"the Word" is now enfleshed.

Midnight! Angels are heard in the clear night winds -
Look around you and see the Child called Wonderful.
He is born in our midst in others' calls to us.
He is born the Only Son - the Father's gift. Be glad!

Christmas 1992

Woodcut by Helen Siegl

Love's Transports

By surprise, love captures our attention.
Not sought, but unsuspecting
We are transformed and life is never quite the same.

Rapture fills us to the brim,
Unequaled or unimagined,
As two souls unite as one, though
not without consternation and struggle.

Then God enters in and touches
As the love of two long for wholeness;
Creative uncreation in the springtime.
Like cocooning butterflies set free
To the becoming fullness of flight
Emerging as the entity unimagined.

Released from being just one,
God blesses the surrender gift
And the union creates through love new life.

Two sons mirror the lives of their creators,
God and "the two" who said "yes"
To Love's invitation of becoming.

Called to openness, two people become one
In thought and deed
And where love is, God is present, too.

For Mary Denise and Vince Curran's
25th Wedding Anniversary
June 5, 1993

Angels

My Guardian Angel is Michael
Of the band of Archangels.
I believe in messengers
Who bring God's words to me enfleshed.

Angels communicate truths
For our own good through others.
Since I am blessed by Michael,
God has sent many Michaels to me.

My life has been a reflection
Of others' presence, strong and powerful,
Visible words of strength and wisdom.
God spoke in persons' virtues to me.

Gradually it was revealed to me
That I was guarded surely
By Heavenly messengers sent
As signs of God's love for me.

Never far away, my messengers
Bring loving words heart-ward.
God seems to say, *"Be open and aware.*
I am passing by as Hope reveals my image."

Guardian, dear! Give light and guide my steps!

Adamstown Retreat
June 20, 1993

Heaven

....

Our imagination reaches out for signs
Of peace and fulfillment for those we love
Who have now crossed into the meadows of home,
The place and state of blessedness.

Gathered in the lightsome presence of God
Joyful souls bathe in the grace of shining gold
And total satisfaction. Love embraces just souls
As angel choirs celebrate new life's victory.

A smiling boy named Paul rests in the Vision
Of complete acceptance for his essence,
A joy-filled soul sent forth by loving hearts
Of those who still wait patiently for understanding.

We, too, can cast our lives and thoughts
Into the loving, waiting arms of a provident God
Who loves us each in our totality of light and dark.
Father, thanks be to you for faith and hope.

But it is LOVE we thank you for, most of all!

For Paul Julio's Third Anniversary into Eternal Life
August, 1993

Choose Life

The incarnated Jesus chose life
That we might have life in its fullness.
Of His abundance in gifting, we have all received.
We sing in joyful strains of our graced life.

Jesus continues His life in being born in us.
Each day we are given choices of life.
We are the life-giving word He speaks of Now.
The heart that embraces all of life around us.

To be life-giver for the homeless and the unborn,
This is our concern as our brother's keeper.
We cannot turn our backs to life's invitation
To be nourishment and fertile ground for others.

Christmas in all of its splendor sheds light
In a world darkened to the pleas for living.
Dignity flows from our graced experiences
To champion the cause for the unwanted and
scorned.

Our call is for loving into being the Christ-Child
Imaged in the unborn and loveless masses haunting
All of us in ghettos, clinics and back streets.
The manger of our hearts hold life most dear.

Come, Lord Jesus! Let Christmas angels chant
That there can be peace on the earth
Only if we own our power to love into being
The lives within our reach and touch.
The light of life is our gift to the world
And that word that empowers us is LOVE.
Thank you, Lord Jesus, for your presence so vivid
That we can see and hear and touch in your poor
ones.

We can be merry, even happy, when we choose You
freely!

Christmas 1993

Seven Years

....

There is magic in the biblical number seven.
And it is with this in mind that I recall
Seven intervening years since you have left us.
Yet not your spirit which lives on in each of us.

You were with us just a few short years
Yet your impact was felt by your ebullient life.
Here, there and everywhere you cast a spell of awe.
We stopped and listened for "joy."

To arrest the busiest of us you came with love.
We could not help but notice your presence
That said it was good to live and to laugh often.
And today, that is what I remember.

I drove through the cemetery today but only paused.
A frozen glance of ice and snow bid me
Only to glance and drive on - a prayer of love
Was on my lips as I once again recalled you.

You are never far away in memories too rich for words!

7th Anniversary of Matt's Homecoming
January 12, 1994

Irish Wedding Blessing

May the love of Christ be reflected in
the three leafed shamrock - Christ's love
and your love intertwined.

May the courage of Patrick, Brendan and
Bridget sustain you in your commitment
to each other - and your faith grow ever
stronger as the days lengthen into years.

May the beauty of Killarney's lakes and dells
Nourish your spirits to embrace the Lord's
own presence in the highlands, the boglands
the heather-fields and Antrim's green glens.

May you come to know in depth the mystery
of each other - opening your hearts to God's
grace which calms the winds, restores the
sun's rays and gently washes away like the
spring rain memories of past wrongs.

May you and your children's children enjoy
the Autumn harvests, fruits of spring plantings
and the reality of love awakening in your hearts
through days and months and years.

When you shall be one in His presence,
may the good you have done for one another
yield seeds of virtue, rising to new life in this
world and in the light of heaven's blue mantle.

Calvert Hall College
April 10, 1994

Stephen M. St. Amant, *Calvert Hall Class of '98*

Jeremy

I hadn't thought of you in a while.
From the bookshelf your name leaped out at me.
I bought the book because of you,
My friend and mentor from the past.

Years gone by when you were there for me.
I cannot believe you are gone from view.
You were vibrant, hearty and whole.
You made everything credible to me.

Part of you lives on in me.
I became a teacher because of you.
I was taken by your smile and goodness,
And in your humanness I understood God.

I so wanted to be like you
As would any boy who loved you as his friend.
I think I've fallen short of the mark.
There was only one like you.

But I am me, imperfect,
And my love for you keeps you alive.
Your words come through me still
As do your gentleness and loving ways.

See how I've kept you in my heart, a lifetime!

Priest Field Retreat
June 29, 1995

Jeremy was my Christian Brother teacher in high school.
He died at the age of 47 as our Provincial.

Song of the Shepherds

Shepherds lived in the region of Bethlehem,
Camping in the fields and keeping night watches.
They each took their turns caring for their flocks
Through the darkness and the cold winds of night.

The glory of God suddenly shown round them
As the Lord's own angel proclaimed to them,
"You have nothing to fear- the news is good news.
Your joy can be shared with all you love."

A Messiah, a Lord, a Savior has come among you.
Born today in David's City is the long awaited One.
He comes as an infant, signed in swaddling clothing,
As God's gift among you in the silence.

The messenger bringing the news, wrapped in light
Was surrounded by hosts of heavenly companions
And they praised God in mighty songs of gladness.
This joy was uncontained, overflowing in peace.

Shepherd boys, stunned and shaken, took it in
And coming to their senses said together,
"We must pursue this favor God has rested on us
And hasten to find the one announced at Bethle-
hem."

And what they found cradled in mystery and wonder,
Was Mary and Joseph with the mangered Babe.
To the simple of heart was revealed
what escaped the wise ones
And they understood a Baby's smiling presence.

And what does all of this mean to us in our day?
Look to the Child, the humble beginnings.
In the purity and singleness of purpose we stand in
awe
Transformed by the beauty and innocence of a Birth.

God's miracle in faith touches the human heart-
be happy!

Calvert Hall College
Christmas 1996

Brother Kevin Strong, F.S.C.

Woodcut by Helen Siegl

About Brother Kevin Patrick Strong, F.S.C.

Written by longtime friend and colleague,
Brother Kevin Stanton, F.S.C.

Brother Kevin Stanton, F.S.C., left;
Brother Kevin Strong, F.S.C., right, 1956.

The words of St. Irenaeus, "the glory of God is in man fully alive," readily come to mind when one attempts to describe the person of Brother Kevin Patrick Strong. Ever since this young man from the hills of western Maryland entered the community of De La Salle Christian Brothers, he has enriched our educational ministries.

For nearly fifty years Brother Kevin has served his religious community in virtually every capacity — from teacher to president, from school counselor to formation counselor, from community leader to provincial councilor. Taking to heart St. John Baptist De La Salle's directive that the brothers be of service to the Church, he has also generously shared his gifts as retreat director, speaker, board member, and hospice volunteer with countless numbers of people beyond our formal educational ministries.

At the root of Brother Kevin's multifaceted life of service is a deep awareness of the presence of a loving God in our lives, and the firm conviction that the Lord's grace empowers us to transform our world through our everyday encounters with others. His appreciation for and desire to affirm the God-given uniqueness and special gifts in each person has enabled him to form close personal friendships with people of all ages and from all walks of life. Those who come to know him immediately become aware of his zest for life as manifested not only in his professional activities, but also in his wit and storytelling skills, his love of song, his painting talents, and his enjoyment of the culinary arts. The wonder of it all is that he manages to share these many talents so effortlessly in his everyday activities.

Over the years, many people have been enriched by their personal encounters with Brother Kevin, as well as inspired by his faith-filled, zealous and joyful approach to life.

This collection of poems affords us added insight into the deeper spiritual perspectives which form the basis of his interior life of prayer and ultimately find reverent expression in his relationships with other people.

Brother Kevin Patrick Strong is a member of the Brothers of the Christian Schools of the Baltimore Province. He is currently the President of Calvert Hall College in Baltimore, Maryland and he has served the cause of Catholic Education for forty-seven years as teacher, counselor, Aspirancy Director, Vice-Principal, Principal and President. Brother Kevin is a native of Cumberland, Maryland where he attended La Salle Institute High School, conducted by the De La Salle Christian Brothers. He entered the order in 1949, just after graduating from high school, and entered the Christian Brothers Novitiate in Ammendale, Maryland. He has studied at La Salle University, the University of Pittsburgh, Temple University, the Catholic University of America, Villanova University and the Tyler Art School.

Brother Kevin Stanton, F.S.C. and Brother Kevin Strong, F.S.C., 1996

Live Jesus in our hearts forever. Live

ber we are in the holy presence of God. Let us remember
holy presence of God. Let us remember we are in the holy
God. Let us remember we are in the holy presence of God.
ber we are in the holy presence of God. Let us remember
holy presence of God. Let us remember we are in the holy
God. Let us remember we are in the holy presence of God.
ber we are in the holy presence of God. Let us remember
holy presence of God. Let us remember we are in the holy
God. Let us remember we are in the holy presence of God.
ber we are in the holy presence of God. Let us remember
holy presence of God. Let us remember we are in the holy
God. Let us remember we are in the holy presence of God.
ber we are in the holy presence of God. Let us remember
holy presence of God. Let us remember we are in the holy
God. Let us remember we are in the holy presence of God.
ber we are in the holy presence of God. Let us remember
holy presence of God. Let us remember we are in the holy
God. Let us remember we are in the holy presence of God.
ber we are in the holy presence of God. Let us remember